THE SYNDICATE

IT'S A GREAT IDEA, YOU CAN BANK ON IT !!!

6th Edition (2013)
Author   Les Field
Editor   Marea Ford

LEGAL DISCLAIMER

Every effort has been made to ensure that this booklet & any associated website are free from error or omissions. However the publisher, the contributors and their respective employees or agents do not accept responsibility for injury, loss or damage occasioned to any person acting or refraining from action as a result of material in this booklet or website whether or not such injury, loss or damage is in anyway due to any negligent act or omission, breach of duty or default on the part of the publisher, the author or their respective employees or agents.

Copyright © 2013 by Leslie Field.   All rights reserved

Table of Contents

The Overview	5
How Does The Syndicate Work?	12
The Stages - Products	17
The Syndicate Books	20
The Syndicate Savings Accounts	27
Deposit Savings Account	27
Deposit Savings Investment	28
The Syndicate Personal Loan Account	29
The Syndicate Home Loan Account	34
The Syndicate Expense Account	32
The Syndicate Investment Account	44
The Syndicate Medical Account	49
The Whole Picture	53
Hey Presto – You've Got Yourself a Syndicate!	59

IT'S A GREAT IDEA, YOU CAN BANK ON IT !!

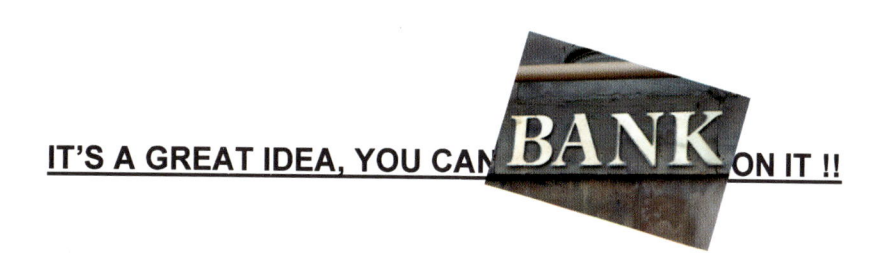

The Overview

In these times of global economic hardship where the dream of home ownership is slipping further away, we need hope for the future more than ever. I can offer you hope in the form of The Syndicate. This concept is for people who feel they are not as financially advanced as they wanted to be at this point in life. It is for those who are scared by the global financial crisis and wonder how they will ever pay off debts or afford to buy a home. It doesn't matter if you're in your 20's or your 50's, if you want to be financially free and believe there must be a safer and more logical way than 'get-rich-quick' and 'pyramid selling' schemes…then this book is definitely for you and those you care about. If you have enough time to do a small amount of reading and planning, you will see a large impact in return for your investment, both in your bank balance and your life.

So what is the **Syndicate**? Well, in its simplest form you could call it a bank, finance company or lending institution. But it is – and can be – so much more than that! I will give you a brief explanation of how it is organised and what it can do for you before going into further detail…

The simple version is that you and a group of friends and/or family work together as a kind of 'savings team', regularly depositing an affordable amount of money in to a joint bank account. Although it may not be a large sum of money each, it grows quickly because there are a number of you working together. Individuals or couples can then begin borrowing it back to pay small debts like credit cards. The borrowed money earns interest, just as it would when loaned from a bank…except now the interest belongs to the group! It's like a community bank working on a microscopic level with only 4-14 people involved. Even more of an impact can be made on the individuals by each Syndicate member sharing the profits derived from interest generated.

As the borrowed funds are paid back and the balance grows, The Syndicate can then continue loaning to other members, and for larger amounts. As debts are cleared and interest earned on the money loaned The Syndicate balance starts to grow very rapidly. It may be difficult to grasp now, but with regular deposits as well as regular repayments and interest accumulating, there is soon enough to begin clearing out larger debts, which then also earn more interest.

A point will be reached where personal debts such as credit cards, car loans and hire purchase agreements for the members are cleared and you can start focusing on their home loans. Yes, home loans. It may seem like the stuff of fairy tales but you will see as you read further through the book that the funds required to begin attacking large debts with confidence will add up quicker than you think. Can you imagine 3 or 4 members (or more!) paying back their home loans at a rate of $800 to $1500 per month just like a bank. This could easily be as much as $6000 p/m coming in, which can then be loaned to the next member (which will earn interest from repayments in addition to the original loan interest which is simultaneously accruing – a kind of cascading waterfall effect as money is accumulated and re-loaned again and again).

Don't forget that in addition to these repayments and interest earnings all members are still making their regular original deposits as well. It is completely realistic and achievable to expect that in as little as 10 - 15 years of working The Syndicate method you can be free from banks and the heavy weight of debt. Imagine, completely debt-free in half the time it normally takes to pay out a home loan alone!!

So How Did This Concept Arise?

The Syndicate began as so many other great ideas and inventions have started – out of the essence of necessity. The origins of this concept began long before the current financial crisis, back in the 1970's. It is now simply the right time to share it.

Some of you may remember December 25, 1974 for more reasons than the usual Christmas celebrations. We were one such family, along with all the other city residents of Darwin, who remember that day more for what was taken away than what was given. My parents, three brothers and I had just survived one of Australia's worst cyclones – Cyclone Tracy. Arriving in the early hours of December 25, 1974, and ravaging all in its path, we were left with nothing except the clothes on our backs, and luckily, our lives. The house, the cars, our furniture and possessions - every last item which had been earned, or borrowed for, was gone or destroyed. Next door was my brother's caravan, sides curled up like a discarded sardine can. Down the street was one of the cars, sandblasted and crushed from the flying debris. And as for the roof of the house and most of the contents, well, their location was anyone's guess.

My father was the typical bread winner and my mother would help out with the odd part time job here and there, such as Avon or Amway. But no matter what they did, they just never seemed to get on top of the money situation. The banks would 'help' by offering them an overdraft facility and made it easy with the good old cheque book. The finance companies which will remain anonymous (although I would love to name them) kept giving Mum and Dad more credit, kept charging the interest and kept asking for the payments each month. At this stage credit cards were not around (until 1974 in Australia).

I was only 17 years old and can remember numerous arguments between my parents, most of which revolved around money, or perhaps the lack of it I should say. You see my Mum was a spender and my Dad was a miser - a bad combination in lots of ways.

Dad would have his secret little stash of money and Mum would just keep spending – not wasting it - but indulging her children as so many parents did and still do! (So in a nice kind of way we had a good childhood).

This had a bittersweet twist because it meant money was always a problem in our family. The problem wasn't getting it - it was paying it back! More than once debt collectors came knocking on our door and we received letters that were frightening from people that were ever so nice to start with. I knew my Mum and Dad had a problem! Well, cyclone Tracy fixed that…it took the whole lot away in one swoop. (Although it did actually take six hours - I said it was all at once but I didn't say it was quick!)

In fact, the problems had only just begun. My parents had purchased the house from the Northern Territory Housing Commission in October of that year. They had decided that after getting through Christmas the next financial goal would be to insure every thing – the house, contents, car and caravan – and start to make tracks financially. Well, come December 26th there was nothing to insure, no walls or roof, no contents to speak of, cars that looked like they had been on the wrong side of a panelbeater, a mangled caravan and the odd dent here and there from the path of the flying hot water system!

We left Darwin (well, we were evacuated) and arrived in Sydney late December. Six weeks later my father whom had been working for QANTAS got offered a role in Brisbane. And so my parents moved us to Brisbane to start again from scratch. New bank accounts, cheque book, overdraft facility, personal loan, home loan, hire purchase loans…right back where we started, only in a completely new town and with even less than we had before (well we had more if you count debt as a possession!).

Now you have probably heard the saying "the definition of insanity is doing the same thing over again and expecting a different outcome". Well in that case, I confess, my parents were totally insane. But then so were the banks because they kept doing the same thing and still are, except they have added a whole new list of products to help you get onboard the credit merry-go-round, such as credit cards, home equity loans, personal loans, investment loans, low doc loans, the list goes on! In some cases banks are even lending more than 100% of the value of the house. And it's not all directly the banks fault, there are also large department and furniture stores helping load us up with debt with their own store credit cards/finance options (most of which are underwritten by finance companies or banks). Oh I could go on - and I probably have - so enough!

We had settled on the North side of Brisbane and my parents were dependant upon the banks and finance companies more than ever. Credit cards were also gaining popularity and becoming more accessible and so of course they had those too. It soon became obvious they were overcommitted. So my two brothers and I began helping here and there, just a little to ease the struggle. We were all working; however my youngest brother was still at school, yet another expense to account for. But none of us knew any better – this is how it has always been!

A Change Was in Store

Little did we know this "monkey see - monkey do" attitude was about to change. A chance conversation with a work colleague brought a revelation. He mentioned that he and his brothers put money into a joint bank account, and then as the bills came in paid them from the accumulated funds. They always kept it in equal shares, which eased the burden and helped to take out the peaks and troughs. All the erratic household bills were paid with one predictable monthly contribution.

This idea intrigued me and got me thinking about whether this sort of idea could help our situation. It was not too long before I had formulated a concept as to how it could work for us. This concept started very simply but evolved and grew over time. It cost us next to nothing to set up - but in return saved us thousands and thousands of dollars (and lots of sleepless nights due to money worries). It can be set up in any state or country with any currency and with as few as three members...and so The Syndicate was born.

The Banks Are All Alike

When I say the banks are all alike, it's not just the banks. It's nearly all lending institutions, credit unions, building societies and finance companies, and any other of the numerous organisations of similar operation. (Though for the sake of brevity I will just refer to them as 'the banks'). The last thing I want to do is to pretend that I know how they all work, because I don't. I am not a financial advisor or banking expert, I am just an everyday person like you. I have no economics degree, no financial qualifications, it's just me and 40 years of experience being a banking customer.

What I do know is that banks have share holders and they want the best return they can get for their money, just as we all do. The lending institution's job is to give their share holders that return, which provides good consumer confidence and the ability for them to lend more people more money. How? They give their shareholders a return by making money in the form of a profit from the sale of their products and services, just like any other business (except they make their money literally out of money).

It all revolves around the Reserve Bank of Australia known as the RBA. The RBA decide how much money to make and how it is distributed throughout the economy. In maintaining the state of the economy the RBA constantly reviews the interest rates. They can reduce public spending by increasing the interest rates or they can increase public spending by reducing the interest rates. The rate that is set by the RBA is known as the official cash rate, and this is the rate that the RBA charges the financial institutions for borrowing the money from the RBA (very simplified version). When the financial institutions loan you the money they charge a higher interest rate, which is where they make their profit. The risk for loaning it to you should you be unable to repay the loan is also factored into the interest rate charged.

So your interest rate is controlled by three main factors: 1.The official cash rate decided from time to time by the RBA, 2.How risky banks feel the economy is in terms of ability to repay, which the banks decide independently and 3 how risky you are, the borrower. So, if for example the economy is slow, the RBA may reduce the cash rate to stimulate spending and if the economy is fairly sound, then the banks will pass on the interest rate reduction to their lenders (and vice versa) In 2012 banks started to break ranks and when the RBA lowered interest rates some banks didn't pass on the full amount! The second way that banks make their money (profit) is by charging fees. They charge fees on transactions, on loan applications, administration charges, valuations, on variations to loans, on ATM usage…the list goes on. In short, there is not much that they don't charge for! Oh, for the good old days when they paid you for the use of your money! Some banks pay only 0.05% per annum on money in savings accounts.

So let's do something about it!

How Does The Syndicate Work?

So, where to begin? Firstly, you must organise your team - the group of people which will form your Syndicate. It can be as few as 3 or as many as 10 or more. It does not need to be fixed, you can add members as you go along or if for some reason you want to reduce the numbers you can do that too. The people in your group can be family members, work mates, friends, or even business associates, or a mixture of these combined.

Once you have at least three people you can open a joint bank account (**Syndicate Savings Bank Account**).where one or two or three people can operate it.

Then, you all agree on an amount which each of you can afford to deposit each week (**Syndicate Payment**). It could be $20, $30, $40, $50 or $100 per week, but it must be an equal amount for each member. Even if some think they could afford more than others, keep it small and simple to start with until you are comfortable with the system (you can always increase the amount).

Say for example there are 6 people all banking $50 per week. That would be 6 people x $50 x 4 weeks= $1200 in the joint account after the first month. Then after 5 months of operation you have $6000. It really does add up quickly!

The success of any team is reliant upon organisation and accountability for the efforts of its members. It is important to keep accurate, regular records of all transactions to and from the **Syndicate Savings Bank Account**. The easiest way is to use a spreadsheet program such as Excel, however there's nothing wrong with using good old pen and paper. **The Syndicate Books** need to show the names of the people in The Syndicate along with how much is paid in each week and what the total balance is.

Once the payment amount has been decided, the account is open and someone is nominated to look after the books, it is a good idea to begin regular meetings. This can be once every month or two just to assess how it's going and see how much has accumulated. It also helps to keep everyone motivated when they can see how rapidly the money is adding up and what a difference their participation is making.

After 4 - 5 months, have a meeting with the primary purpose of lending some money to a Syndicate member. At the meeting you find out who has a debt with a credit card - most likely every one! – and choose the one that has the least amount owing and pay it off (**Syndicate Personal Loan Account**). But when you do, there is an agreement that the person whose credit card is paid off will pay it back into The Syndicate joint account (Syndicate Savings Account), with interest.

The debt which was originally earning interest for the banks will now earn the Syndicate interest instead (this is using your debts as personal financial leverage). But because your Syndicate is friendly, it is going to charge at a rate 1% less than the rate previously being paid to the bank. So if the member was paying 17% p.a. the Syndicate charges 16% p.a. if they are paying 15% p.a. the Syndicate charges 14% p.a. Some credit cards (most) are charging 21% on cash advances so if your syndicate member is paying this high rate then you should pay theirs out first and do them and the syndicate a favour. The syndicate could earn a higher rate and grow quicker. The interest is charged on the balance at the end of each month.

Now you may be wondering how this helps the person paying off their card. You see, if there are six Syndicate members they are each going to get 1/6 of the interest back later, and in the meantime The Syndicate is swelling with the funds to allow the next person to pay off a debt. The interest paid is actually an investment as all the money comes back to the Syndicate members to use instead of in the bank's pocket to keep. Without The Syndicate you would have no choice but to pay the interest anyway – this is just a method of letting the normal banking processes work for *you*. Don't stress about the details at this stage, there's plenty more to explain and once you make a start it will all become clear and quite easy.

Example

The Syndicate pays $4000 off John's credit card and his rate with the bank was 16% p.a. So The Syndicate is going to charge 15% p.a. (16%-1%) and now divide by 12 because it's being charged monthly. So let's say at the end of the month John has paid $300 off his new Syndicate loan. He now has a balance of $3700. So the interest will be 15% divided by 12, which equals 1.25% per month. If he has a balance of $3700 X 1.25% = $46.25 in interest, this is added on to his Syndicate Personal Loan balance. This makes his new balance $3746.25 and so The Syndicate has made its first $46.25. (This is $46.25 the credit card company did not get!)

So how does the picture look after sixth months? Well, there was $6000 in the **Syndicate Savings Account** of which $4000 was loaned out to John. This leaves a balance of $2000, plus the $300 that John has paid back to The Syndicate. So that's now a balance of $2300 back in the **Syndicate Savings Account** and still everybody has continued to pay the $50 per week ($1200 for the month all together) so the balance is back to $3500. Then after one more month the balance would be $5000 ($3500 + $1200+ $300). The Syndicate can now loan some more to the next person, let's call him Frank.

So Frank borrows $2000 and agrees to pay back $200 p/m. Lets also assume for simplicity that the interest rates are the same as before. So now at the end of nine months, John has made 4 payments of $300 and the second borrower Frank has made 2 payments of $200. The Syndicate has loaned out a total of $6000, but with repayments on loans plus the regular contributions the account balance is at $6400 and The Syndicate has earned about $208 in interest. The total value of The

Syndicate after 9 months is just over $11,000. What have you achieved? Well, you have earned 15% p.a. on your money, approximately $208. You've paid two credit cards off and you still have $6400 in the bank ready to do some thing else with - and there's more money still coming in! Take a look at table 1 below.

Table 1 Remember this is only 6 people paying $50 per week!!

	Deposit Per month 6x$50	John's Loan	John's payments	Frank's Loan	Frank's payments	Combined interest earned	Bank Bal
Month 1	1200						1200
Month 2	1200						2400
Month 3	1200						3600
Month 4	1200						4800
Month 5	1200	4000					2000
Month 6	1200		300			46.25	3500
Month 7	1200		300	2000		43.07	3000
Month 8	1200		300		200	62.36	4700
Month 9	1200	This would be the balance inc int	300	This would be the balance inc int	200	56.89	6400
Balances	$10800	$2963.79	$1200	$1644.78	$400	$208.57	=$11008.57

**If you add up John's and Franks loan balance which includes the interest earned and add this to the bank balance you have $11008.57 in total assets or a growth of $208.57

You can see from the example above (this is the **Syndicate Loan Product**) that it does not take long to have a reasonable amount of money in the account earning good interest. It is so gentle that you don't realise how fast it grows and how effectively your money can work for you until you look at it spread out in a table like this. It looks like you are earning an income by way of interest but you are actually saving money. As your Syndicate matures and you introduce more products (as explained later) you will save more and more money - it will literally grow overnight!

As the money starts to accumulate (and it will) you will find that you have too much money available to pay off the credit cards or personal loans. Now you really move in to the realms of the banks (**The Syndicate Home Loan**).

Of the members that you have in The Syndicate you decide whose home loan is the lowest and start to pay lump sums off the chosen home loan, working it in a very similar way to the personal loans. The only difference is that in most cases the loan cannot be paid out in full so you will need to do it in steps. I will go into more detail later as to how you choose which will be the best loan to start paying off first.

It's not hard to imagine just like the credit cards or personal loans, if you start paying your home loan back to The Syndicate, you could be paying back as much as $1200 a month (or more, depending on the size of your loan). This is in addition to what every body else is paying back by way of their loans, plus the normal Syndicate weekly amount which continues regardless. It can quite easily amount to $3000 to $5000 or more in total going back into The Syndicate **Savings Account** each month, thereby becoming available for someone else in The Syndicate to borrow or pay towards their home loan. If this does not excite you, you may need to check your pulse!

The Stages - Products

As our Syndicate progressed through time it evolved and grew. We created new products that made our life easier and more fun, but most of all put us in control of our money instead of the banks or finance companies having us on a string. It was not hard, it was not complicated and best of all it made our family stronger and closer.

There are four basic stages (Products), which are:
1) **The Syndicate Book**
2) **The Syndicate Savings Account**
3) **The Syndicate Personal Loan account**
4) **The Syndicate Home Loan Account**

There are three Optional Products, which are:
5) **The Syndicate Expense Account (semi optional)**
6) **The Syndicate Investment account**
7) **The Syndicate Medical Account**

How and Where to Begin…

day	dollars	day	dollars
1	.01	16	327.68
2	.02	17	655.36
3	.04	18	1,310.72
4	.08	19	2,621.44
5	.16	20	5,242.44
6	.32	21	10,485.76
7	.64	22	20,971.52
8	1.28	23	41,943.04
9	2.56	24	83,886.08
10	5.12	25	167,772.2
11	10.24	26	335,544.3
12	20.48	27	671,088.6
13	40.96	28	1,342,177
14	81.92	29	2,684,355
15	163.84	30	5,368,709

Table 2 (1 cent doubled for 30 days)

For those that don't know, Oak trees didn't just appear, they all grew from an acorn. So you need to visualise an acorn and now an Oak tree. Firstly, one does not look like the other and when you evaluate size - well there is no comparison! And the same is true for your Syndicate, it will start off so small you will think that it is not capable of huge growth. But it is and you will soon be surprised at what your Acorn has grown up to be! It reminds me of that age-old question – "Would you like a million dollars straight up or would you rather 1 cent doubled every day for a month?" Most people would immediately say "Give me the million dollars!!" But little do they realise that 1 cent doubled every day for 30 days equals over 5 million dollars!!! ($5,368,709 to be exact - see table 2). Now I'm not saying you will do it in 30 days, but you will be surprised by how fast The Syndicate will grow!!

Choosing the people

So to start off with, the seed (or Acorn) must be planted. As you are the one that has bought this book, it will most likely be you who plants the seed. And just the same as any other seed, you will need to obtain the right mix around it for the best result. Whilst an Acorn requires the best mix of nutrients, moisture and sunlight for its growth – the mix you are looking for is people. The mix of people is probably the hardest part. They need to be trustworthy and trusting, they need to have a regular income (or at least some disposable income), they need to have debts (without being on the verge of bankruptcy) and they need dedication. They need to be like-minded to you. Now don't jump to the conclusion that family members are going to be the best candidates, this is often not the case! Nor is it necessarily true for best friends. But it can be any mix of these people, or as previously mentioned even work mates or business associates, just as long as the mix is right. Please keep in mind that it is like a partnership and in the long term there will be some large sums of money involved. I certainly do not recommend forming a Syndicate with casual acquaintances, but none the less it will be your choice.

Voting

Once you have selected the members of your Syndicate it is important to note that all members have equal voting rights when it comes to decision making time and at voting time. It is best that if a husband and wife or partner are part of your Syndicate then together they have the decision making or voting right of only one person. As you can imagine if your Syndicate has 3 couples and 3 singles it would be unfair to allow the partners to vote individually. It could become very biased very quickly!

Another important rule to help avoid arguments (one of the single biggest risks), is that the outcome is not decided by a 'majority rules' type of system, it must be unanimous. All members need to agree to the decision; even if only one person disagrees then it is up to the rest to convince that person why they should agree, otherwise not go ahead with the request. This will save many, many arguments and potential "I-told-you-so"s in the future. The rule of 'what goes around comes around' plays a big part in your Syndicate. Next month it may be you who does not want something to happen and the group will have to honour your wishes too.

This rule also applies to partners within The Syndicate. If Frank is voting and his wife does not agree with the issue at hand then he must convince her to agree or visa versa. It is not her place to argue her point with everybody else (it may be that the wife is The Syndicate member with the voting rights in which case the reverse will be true). Whichever the case a couple with the voting rights of one person must be united in agreement and decide their vote between themselves. It is worth repeating here that the mind set of "all for one and one for all" will almost always guarantee a long and successful Syndicate. The aim is to make life easier and more comfortable, not to lose friends or fall out with family members or partners.

The Syndicate Books

So, you have formulated your Syndicate group from your family members (e.g. 2 brothers & 2 sisters, 1 brother & 1 sister & parents or an uncle or aunt), colleagues or business partners from work or just a few good close friends. Of course the more you have the faster it will grow, but this also means more people who must all agree on the decisions. These decisions may be whose loan to pay off first, whose house to start paying off, along with how much you can all afford to regularly contribute and so on. Also, one person will need to look after the book work / paper work which will become a bigger and more time consuming task as the numbers grow. So this is an instance where the concept of 'the more the merrier' might not apply. Ideally a minimum of four or five up to about seven or eight members generally works well.

The next step is to have the first meeting. It does not have to be a formal meeting and you don't have to take minutes, although it might be helpful in the future to see what was decided at which meeting. There doesn't need to be a president/chairperson or a secretary and you absolutely don't need a boss of any kind! What is needed is a spokesperson or someone to help lead the way (in most cases it will be the person that introduces the idea to the team to start with – most likely **You**!). As you would expect the spokesperson needs to understand the concept, needs to be able to listen, adjudicate if necessary and stay calm 99.9% of the time. Of all the times I have been asked if it was difficult to get The Syndicate started, the answer was a resounding no. The hardest part was keeping the peace - The Syndicate took care of itself - it was the members that needed the guidance! So again it is helpful to keep this in mind when you are deciding on the numbers.

The first item on the agenda is to decide which bank to open the joint account with. When deciding on the bank, credit union or building society to use, you will need to consider the ease of dealing with them directly and indirectly (particularly in regard to internet access and accessibility of transaction history). Whilst interest rates are important (at the time of writing 3-5% p.a.) it is not the only consideration. What the banking institution can do for The Syndicate as a group later on might be worth thinking about too.

Assuming that you have agreed on a banking institution (and you haven't decided it all too hard on the first meeting!), you need to collect some money to open the account with. I suggest that you all put in just $5 or $10 to start with (our Syndicate started with just $1 each - yep that's right, just $4 in total!). Depending on how many members you have in The Syndicate, you may need to talk to the bank and decide the type of account which is most suitable (e.g. a savings account or target account, as well as whether it is in the form of a joint account or trust account).

Now with all that in place, you need to be able to record where the money is, how much there is and who paid what and when. This is easy because everyone is making a Syndicate payment of the same amount at approximately the same time to the same place. For example, if you have all agreed to pay $30 per week this is the **Syndicate Payment** amount. However, some may pay weekly, some fortnightly and some monthly, depending on pay cycles, which does make it a little more complex. Take a look at Table 3 below.

Table 4 mixed payments cycle

Payment decided	weekly	fortnightly	Monthly**
$30	$30.00	$30x52/26=$60.00	$30x52/12=$130.00
$40	$40.00	$40x52/26=$80.00	$40x52/12=$173.33

** Most people think monthly = weekly x 4 but it is actually weekly x 4.3333 (there is a little more than 4 weeks in every month so you are finding the average over 12 months ie 52 wk / 12 months)

As you can see it is very straightforward if everybody pays at the same interval, but it can get quite messy and difficult to monitor if everyone wants to pay at different times. There are two solutions to this problem. The first solution is very easy - you all decide on the same interval i.e. weekly, fortnightly or monthly. The second solution may seem complicated but is tied in with other processes of The Syndicate later. This second solution is to set up a **Syndicate Loan Account** and transfer the **Syndicate Payment** across to **Syndicate Books** each month from the Loan Account. This process can be a bit confusing, please read through the following example and table carefully, re-reading if you need to – just hang in there and it will all become clear!

For example: Karen pays weekly and at the end of the month has paid $120 (4 x $30) and the next month $160 (5 x $30) because the first month had 4 pays and the second month had 5 pays so in total Karen has paid $280. Now Mark wants to pay monthly on the last day of each month, so from his loan account for the first month The Syndicate deducts $120 which will match Karen's payment. Then Mark will make a monthly payment of $130 to the **Syndicate Loan Account** minus the $120 deducted from the loan account, which will leave him a spare $10. The following month The Syndicate deducts $160 from his loan account which matches Karen's amount and leaves Mark at minus $150 ($10-160= -$150) Mark then makes a monthly payment of $130 to the account that leaves Mark at minus -$20 (-$150+130= -$20) and so it goes on like a see-saw up and down, but on the 12th month Mark and Karen have paid the same amount (Karen 52 x $30 = $1560 and Mark has paid 12 x $130 = $1560). Confused? Don't be, a picture is worth a thousand words! See the following two tables:

Table 5 Typical Syndicate Books sample page

Date	Mark	Karen	Frank	John	Comment	Balance
Oct 5		30	30	60	payment	120
Oct 12		30	30		payment	180
Oct 19		30	30	60	payment	300
Oct 26	120*	30	30		payment	480
Nov 2		30	30	60	payment	600
Nov 9		30	30		payment	660
Nov 16		30	30	60	payment	780
Nov 23		30	30		payment	840
Nov 30	150*	30	30	60	payment	1110
Dec 7		30	30		payment	1170
Dec 14		30	30	60	payment	1290
Dec 21		30	30		payment	1350
Dec 28	120*	30	30	60	payment	1590
					↓↓↓↓↓↓	
Balance	390	390	390	420	→→→	1590 this is the cross balance check

In the final Balance row Mark, Karen & Frank have now all paid the same amount. John is $30 ahead which levels out after 6 months. *Remember Mark's money is coming out of his **Syndicate Loan Account** which would look like table 5:

Table 6 Typical Syndicate loan Sample sheet (for Mark)

Date	Description	Loan Amount	Interest 1% p/m	Payment	Balance owing
Oct 15	Payment in			130	-130.00
Oct 26	Syndicate	120.00			-10.00
Oct 30	Interest		-.10		-10.10
Nov 15	Payment in			130	-140.10
Nov 30	Syndicate	150.00			9.90
Nov 30	Interest		.09		9.99
Dec 15	Payment in			130	-120.01
Dec 28	Syndicate	120.00			-.01
Dec 30	Interest		0		-.01
Cross Check		390 plus	-.01 minus	390 equals	-.01

Page 24

There are a couple of points to make here. First of all, you must be fair: if a Syndicate member owes The Syndicate money then Syndicate charges them interest. If, on the other hand, The Syndicate owes *them* money, then The Syndicate must likewise pay them interest (that's why there are a couple of negative or 'minus' interest amounts). You will notice in the above example that Mark earns a little interest and then pays a little interest but it comes close to balancing out (I have rounded to the nearest whole cent).

It is important that when the interest is calculated and the books are balanced (explained in detail later) that you account for every cent. This not only helps the books balance but it makes you aware of what is happening in detail, hence reducing errors. HONESTY and carefulness is the only way The Syndicate will work because everybody must give trust and be trustworthy in return. This is why on the last row I have a simple cross-check. By adding all the columns, totalling those at the bottom and then adding the last row (watch out for minus numbers) it will equal the final balance.

As previously discussed, it makes it much easier if all Syndicate members pay the same amount at the same time. But, if your syndicate can be flexible it makes it easier on the other members individually too. A loan account will need to be set up for each member at some stage anyway if they are going to pay out a loan (such as a credit card), which is the whole purpose to start with. It just means that the loan account is active sooner and requires some more entries. I will come back to the **Syndicate Loan Account** later.

The whole idea of The Syndicate **Book** is to record how much everybody has contributed. If some of the members have not got **Syndicate Loan Account**s or **Syndicate Investment Account**s then it is the only place you can record their payment as an individual.

Let's Take a Break

I'm sure that most people have heard the saying 'There is no such thing as something for nothing'. Well, this is certainly the case with setting up and running The Syndicate. No Effort = No Result. Within The Syndicate the rules apply equally. The Syndicate cannot loan the money out if there isn't any deposited by way of either the Syndicate payments or loan repayments. So it is obvious that ability to repay the loan must also exist before The Syndicate lends the money.

Although the idea is to help family and friends by working together, if The Syndicate dissolves because of unpaid debt nobody will be helped at all – and indeed some damage could be done to relationships along the way! The Syndicate should also operate with complete transparency. At any one time each member should be able to see how much is in The Syndicate either by way of contributions or loan repayments, as well as how much has been borrowed or loaned and to whom. The Syndicate is much like a company, a business, a club or a machine - it runs best when it is well organised, well maintained, and with a duty of care to all members.

Ok, Breaks Over

So we have looked at the **Syndicate Book.** This is the book where the weekly, fortnightly or monthly payments are recorded. It really just depicts who is in The Syndicate, for how long, how much each person has paid in at the regular intervals and the total of the contributions at any one time. It would look very similar to the table 4 layout. One of the reasons that a **Syndicate Loan Account** is set up is to make contributions for members that want to pay at different intervals. Another use is that when a member can't make a payment due to lack of work or illness, or one month they may have an unexpected financial need, they can continue to have the contribution made via the loan account, thereby keeping everything equal (working similar to an overdraft).

The Syndicate Savings Accounts

Part A – Deposit Savings Account

So you already know that the money that's deposited must go to a joint account or trust account of some kind. This account can be operated by more than <u>one</u> person - you should not let too many operate the account it will be too confusing. As previously mentioned you will need to decide on the type of financial institution that you are going to use.

The general day to day savings will need a standard type of account and as discussed earlier interest rates are not the most important factor although of course it needs to be considered. There are normally more transactions of money going in than coming out, certainly in the first couple of years. Many banks charge for transactions, so the cost of these transactions needs to be weighed up against the ease of use (withdrawal limits, ATM machines).

Internet banking is a must today and I'm sure all banks have this facility. If, however, The Syndicate chooses one that doesn't offer an online service, there is essentially nothing wrong with this. It just means the monitoring of the accounts and payments will be more difficult and not as easily accessed (viewed only) by all members (should you choose this).

The **Syndicate Savings Account** is used for one thing and one thing only - Syndicate transactions. Like any other organisation, never mix business with personal transactions. At times it will be a task to keep track of normal Syndicate transactions let alone any stray ones. Not to mention that the account is based around trust i.e. people have put trust in the operator to use it as specified. As per standard accounting practices, all bank statements should be kept and filed.

Part B – Deposit Savings Investment

In the early days as the money is building up (providing all Syndicate members are quite happy to leave it there) and depending on your long term goals, it may reach $5,000 to $10,000 in the account. If The Syndicate's intention is to build up a decent deposit towards paying home loans only, then it would be well worth opening an investment account and taking advantage of the higher interest rates on offer. These can be fixed term accounts e.g. 6 months or 12 months. An extra income of $600 interest over 12 months on $10,000 in The Syndicate will help everybody.

As with the entire Syndicate process, the philosophy is that 'One in the hand is worth two in the bush'. By this I mean it is one thing to invest the money and get a nominal return of 5%-6% p.a. on your money which is a positive and calculable result. It is quite a different thing to invest that money where returns are uncertain, such as in the share market. Yes, there may be 'two birds' waiting in the share market, but there may also be no birds because of a bushfire – hands up if you have heard of a stock market crash? Besides, The Syndicate is not a superannuation scheme, nor is it intended to be extremely long term (30 years or so at the very most). The aim is for each and every member to be debt-free and own their home outright. Then afterwards if you want to invest in shares or bonds and take greater risks you can do so.

It's worth mentioning here that if you have questions or are not sure about something along the way, ask yourself "What would the bank do?". Follow their lead, because The Syndicate is essentially your own bank!

The Syndicate Personal Loan Account

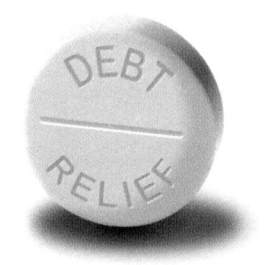

I broached on the subject of the **Syndicate Personal Loan Account** earlier when discussing the **Syndicate Book** and making payments. I must admit this is my favourite part. This is where I saw the first real changes and the power of The Syndicate process. It's where I saw The Syndicate start to grow and our lives start to get easier. As the name implies the **Syndicate Personal Loan Account** is for your personal loans or credit cards. It helps take the bumps out of your financial roller coaster. You can stop living week-to-week and start seriously planning ahead.

Basically it works like this: as the money grows in the **Syndicate Savings Account** the most you can earn there is 4-6% p.a. Why would you have money sitting there earning little interest when at the same time you have a credit card that you are paying 16-17% p.a. on to the bank? The many credit card companies would like to thank you for not asking this question, as this is what makes them their money. You will find most banks would rather give you a credit card than a personal loan. This is because they make more money and with less risk.

So what The Syndicate does is to loan the money to you instead. And just like the credit card company The Syndicate is going to charge you interest but with two differences. Firstly, The Syndicate is going to give you a discount rate (there needs to be some personal incentive too!) and secondly, unlike the credit card company who charge you compound interest calculated on the daily balance, The Syndicate is going to charge you interest on the monthly balance only.

The discount you give on the interest rate depends on which option you all agree on to start with and what best suits your Syndicate's needs. For instance, say The Syndicate voted that the discount rate was going to be 2% p.a. less than the rates being charged by the banks. Therefore Syndicate member Mark, who currently pays 18% p.a. on his credit card, would now get 16% p.a. through The Syndicate; Karen's rate on her personal loan will drop from 15% p.a. to 13% p.a., and Frank's car loan at 13% p.a. will now be just 11% p.a. But then John might need to borrow $2000 to pay his rates that have just come in - what rate would you charge him? And are all these rates fair at a 2% reduction across the board or should it be voted case-by-case?

Well, what you decide is up to The Syndicate vote - and remember - it must be unanimous! Members must vote (and it may be a good idea to do this early on) and agree on the rates to be charged for loan pay-outs as well as new Syndicate Loans (i.e. loans for new purchases or payments such as John's rates bill). This should be at a competitive rate to discourage members from putting debts onto credit cards and then getting the credit card paid out by The Syndicate. Remember, the whole idea is to discourage the use and dependence on loans and credit cards and to form new habits towards financial control and freedom. Likewise, members must not abuse The Syndicate system and expect The Syndicate to continually cover for poor budgeting…The Syndicate is not your personal piggy bank!

The Agreed Rate of Interest

The purpose of The Syndicate is to help each member become financially free from the banks and to own their own homes. To be able to reach that goal The Syndicate must generate a substantial income (just like the banks have been doing for years!).

Apart from the regular Syndicate payments, interest is the only other way to quickly and safely gather the required capital growth. You need to have a closer look at this double-edged sword…you are saving interest *and* growing your Syndicate by using it instead of the banks. You are profit-sharing your own interest payments while you save money – awesome!!

Now consider this scenario: you have a personal car loan for $11000 and you were masterful in negotiating an exceptionally good interest rate of 11% p.a. over 5 years. This means in the **first** month you will pay about $101 in interest alone. How much of that $101 will you get back? The answer is zero, of course, because the bank gets it all! (We're going to keep this simple and not take into account possible tax deductions if the vehicle is for business purposes. The Syndicate is really for personal use, not as a business-support scheme. By the same token it is now yours to do as you wish and as The Syndicate votes).

Now lets assume that you get the loan paid out by The Syndicate upon the condition that 12% p.a. interest will be charged. The first month's payment is slightly more at $110, but how much do you get back? The answer is that it all goes to The Syndicate of which you have a ¼ share (providing there are four members), so you get back $27.50, which means that really you are only paying 9% p.a. If you want to make it complicated you could say that by leaving your share in The Syndicate (which you will do anyway) when it gets loaned out again and earns 12% p.a. on the $27.50 which is $3.30 then you are actually getting back $33.80 of your original interest of $110.00 so then you're only paying 8.31% p.a. Without going on any further it's plain to see that it's in your best interest (no pun intended) to borrow the money from The Syndicate. With this information in mind please revisit your thoughts on the discounts and interest rates The Syndicate will offer…

In the case of paying out a credit card or personal loan, once the loan has been fully paid back to The Syndicate, any subsequent loan which is for a new purchase or payment (i.e. not paying out an existing loan) would be at the agreed general Syndicate interest rate e.g. 12% p.a. At the time of writing personal loans were around 14% pa but depending when you read this they can be as low as 6-7% or as high as 16-17%.

The **Syndicate Loan Account** can also be used to take the troughs and peaks out of your financial situation. Let's say that your rates and electricity are due at the same time, then you remember the registration for the car is also due in a few days – that's a bad start to the month!! Normally you would juggle the finances, maybe pay some bills on the credit card and only pay 6 months of registration (incurring an additional $30-$40 for not paying annually – it's funny that when you can least afford it they charge you more!!). On the electricity account you get a 3% discount for paying on time as an incentive, but you just don't see how you can meet their timeframe. So you're spending more money in the long run because you haven't got enough to keep up with this horrible month! So instead you can borrow the money from The Syndicate, pay them all on time and get the cheapest rates and biggest discounts. You can then pay the money back to The Syndicate when you get paid, or over the next month or two, or even six months if you need to.

So what interest rate does The Syndicate charge for a loan that was not pre-existing? Again this is a decision that The Syndicate must make collectively, remembering that you need to be competitive in the market place while being fair as well. My suggestion is 12% p.a. There are a couple of reasons for this: 1) In most cases it is competitive and reasonable compared to similar banking products 2) It is easy to calculate because 12% p.a. is 1% per month so a $5000.00 dollar loan is $50 p/m interest. A $7549.00 loan is $75.49 p/m interest - all you are doing is moving the decimal point two places to the left and 3) Keeping it simple makes it easier to spot any errors and it gives each member an easy understanding of how much interest they are going to pay.

In summary, I suggest discounting the existing credit cards or loans by 2% down to a minimum of 12% p.a. For example, 18% down to 16% p.a., 16% down to 14% p.a., etc. but 13% only down to 12% p.a. - this way The Syndicate members are always earning at least 12% p.a. on money that has been loaned for personal loans and the member is still getting some relief on their card interest rate. For loans that are not pre-existing just charge 12% p.a. It keeps it all nice and simple!

Now I'll show you how to set The Syndicate loan up. Personally, I found an Excel spreadsheet the easiest way to do this. For those who prefer a pen-and-paper approach then a thin pre-ruled accounting book will also work well. Alternatively, you can generate a page on the computer and print it out to fill in for each member by hand if you find that easier. I have included a blank sheet in the Appendix; you may want to use that as your template and can photocopy it if you wish or you can buy a copy of the XL spread sheet from me, see my web page www.thesyndicatebook.com or at the back of this book.

Basically the page will need to include 6 columns and look similar to the following–

Table 7 Sample of Syndicate Loan Account

Date	Name of Borrower: Frank Smart / Description or Comment	Loan Amount	Payment Amount	Interest Rate 12%pa	Balance
3/5/09	Paid Visa card	4500.00			4500.00
22/5/09	Payment		200.00		4300.00
31/5/09	Interest			43.00	4343.00
22/6/09	Payment		200.00		4143.00
30/6/09	Interest			41.43	4184.43
22/7/09	Payment		250.00		3934.43
31/7/09	Interest			39.34	3973.77
Cross Check Totals	Loan amounts – payments+ Interest= Balance	4500.00	650.00	123.77	$3973.77 it Balances with above

Most of the columns are self explanatory; just make sure in the interest rate column that the interest rate is shown as either per annum or per month and when entering the amounts use cents. At the bottom do your cross-check to make sure you have done your maths right. Don't panic if it's not right the first time, just go back through the figures and let common sense guide you.

A loan account page must be created for each member as they incur a loan. There is only one personal loan per member; if they incur other expenses that they want to add on then that will be at the current agreed interest rate, which remains constant until they reduce the balance to zero. This acts as a kind of incentive, and stops members from having 2 or 3 loans and getting themselves too deep in debt. It's also worth mentioning that the member should restrain from using their credit card as much as possible or they can easily become overwhelmed – owing The Syndicate *and* the bank. It should be mandatory that a minimum payment is paid off the loan every month of at least twice what the interest is for that month e.g. if the interest is $48.00 then the minimum payment is $96.00. This way there is an assurance that the loan is reducing adequately over time. Of course there is no limit to repayments and additional or larger repayments should be encouraged.

The Syndicate Home Loan Account

So by now The Syndicate is bubbling along nicely. The Syndicate has money coming in from a couple of sources like the monthly Syndicate payment, a few Syndicate personal loans as well money from any investment bank accounts that The Syndicate has set up, as well as some sources that have not been discussed yet. If everybody is doing as they should and watching their spending, The Syndicate's personal loan payments will be coming in quite quickly and adding up to considerable money in The Syndicate Savings Account.

Having money in the bank is great, but you are only earning maybe 4 -5% p.a. on that money. (Don't forget you should declare that income as a taxable income divided by the number of members in your group – this is for the interest earned on money in The Syndicate Savings and Investment Accounts only as this is derived from an outside source [paid to your account by your nominated banking institution] and is therefore taxable. Do not include the interest earned lending the money to your own members and yourself as this is your own money to start with - interest is paid and earned within your group only).

You can only loan so much out as personal loans, so what next? Well a lot depends on how much is in the bank account, which members have home loans, and for how much! It's meeting time again, the bank balances are growing and so it's time to put your thinking caps on! Lets say your Syndicate has $10-15,000 in the bank and some of The Syndicate members have home loans ranging from $100,000 (the lucky ones) up to $300,000 - $400,000 or more (the stressed ones). Let's also assume that you are paying 6% p.a. on your home loan[1].

At this point it is important to mention that if you have two loans over the same period of time and at the same interest rate, then the total interest will be the same as if you had one loan for the whole amount, as per the following table:

Table 8 The Mathematical Law of Distribution

	Loan Amount	Interest rate	Interest in $	comment
(a)	$60,000	(c) 6%	$3600	Each loan
(b)	$40,000	(c) 6%	$2400	Each loan
(a+b)	$100,000	(c) 6%	$6000	Total loan
(a + b) × c = a × c + b × c				

---

[1] At the time of writing interest rates were around 5 ½ to 6 % in a very stressed market

This is called the Law of Distribution…but why on earth would I want to tell you that? Well, it's important to understand this law because it plays an enormous part in understanding how the **Syndicate Home Loan** works. It is obvious that The Syndicate is not going to have $100,000 in the bank until much later on in The Syndicate's life span. So when the funds start to build up if you can earn more interest by lending the money to start paying off member's home loans (as compared to the money sitting in the bank accumulating at 4% p.a. interest and not directly helping anyone) then you should do so.

So, which loan are you going to start with? Well, I'll explain how you decide that a little later but for now I'll describe how the Syndicate Home Loan works.

A person that has a mortgage on their home is paying something like 6 or 7% p.a. over 30 years. So on a $100,000 loan that equals approximately $665 per month, a $200,000 loan would be $1331 per month (twice what $100,000 loan was) and so on. Because the existing home loan is with a lending institution and unless they can pay out the whole amount they will have to continue to make their monthly repayments to that institution as well. So although they borrow the money from The Syndicate they would not be paying any back until they have completely paid their existing bank loan in full. Even if they had surplus money they would be better paying that directly off their home loan rather than to The Syndicate.

The money that The Syndicate loans them in effect becomes an interest-only, no-repayment loan, that is, they are only charged interest on the balance of the loan with The Syndicate until they pay out the bank completely. Once they are clear of the bank they can start making regular payments (principal and interest) towards the balance with The Syndicate. The interest that The Syndicate charges is exactly the same as the bank was charging. This is different to The Syndicate Personal Loan because of the extended time frames involved and the larger amounts. The interest is a variable rate linked to their current bank loan rate, which means that if their bank puts the interest rate up then The Syndicate matches it, if the bank lowers interest rates then The Syndicate does the same, again unlike the Syndicate personal loan which is fixed. In the current market, banks offer various products with different interest rates such as honeymoon rates, interest-only rates, investors' rates and then your standard run-of-the-mill rate. Once the portion of the home loan that was with the bank has been finalised, that is the syndicate has taken over all of the home loan then the loan with the syndicate will be like a normal home loan where you make payments and some pays off the interest and some pays of the principle loan. It will then reflect the standard current home loan rate, and remain variable.

We found that by matching their current bank home loan rates it keeps it completely fair within any economy. In setting the interest rate you don't have to match it exactly to two decimal places. A bank might have an interest rate of 6.48% or 6.52% then you would make it 6.5%. The rate is only varied when it has changed by a full 0.1% which saves having to make an adjustment every time the bank makes a move. Please note these are only my suggestions and your Syndicate might decide otherwise. But keeping it relative does help - a loan of $20,000 with a difference in interest rate between what the bank charges and The Syndicate charges of 0.05% p.a. only makes approximately $1.00 per month variation. It may be that your member is charged slightly more for 6 months and then makes a saving for 6 months, but keeping decimals to one place certainly makes things simpler. For example, if the bank is charging 6.35% p.a. then The Syndicate could charge either 6.3% p.a. (which is less by 0.05%) or The Syndicate could charge 6.4% p.a. (which is greater by 0.05%). Our Syndicate always worked in the favour of the member, so in this instance would charge 6.3% p.a.

See table 8.

Table 9 Difference between interest rates Bank vs Syndicate

Bank % rate	Syn % rate	% difference	Savings on p/m on $100,000
6.00	6.00	.00	$0.00
6.05	6.00	- .05	- $4.16
6.10	6.10	.00	$0.00
6.13	6.10	- .03	- $2.50
6.17	6.20	+ .03	+$2.50
6.22	6.20	- .02	- $1.66
6.25	6.20	- .05	- $4.16
6.35	6.30	- .05	- $4.16

Yet again I emphasise that a 'big picture' attitude must be adopted to make this work well. In this case by charging 6.3% p.a. on $20,000 you have earned The Syndicate $1260 extra for the year in interest but it is also $1260 the bank doesn't get (*yes!!*) As The Syndicate home loan starts to reach $100,000 your Syndicate is earning (or technically saving) $6300.00 per year in interest and that's only on $100,000 - imagine a $300,000 loan (banks don't get their lavish buildings from selling raffle tickets!)

Singapore Bank

Again it is a positive double edged sword, because as The Syndicate is saving the extra money the member is making a bigger dent in the principal amount they owe the bank. The objective is that in a couple of years The Syndicate is able to take over the entire home loan from the bank. As soon as that happens The Syndicate member then starts paying off The Syndicate home loan with principal and interest included. This is paid at exactly the same amount per month that they were paying the bank. For example, if they were paying $700 per month before, then likewise that will be their minimum repayment to The Syndicate. Please notice I have written minimum repayment for a reason: they are free to and in fact encouraged to make larger repayments. This not only helps them become debt-free sooner, but it assists the other members as there is more money coming in to start to pay off their mortgages as well!

So back to deciding whose loan to start with first…At your meeting you discover that Frank has the lowest outstanding amount on his home loan, lets say $100,000, and the next highest is Karen's at $170,000 and Mark's is at $300,000. Now it's not just a matter of flipping a coin, there is a very easy but important strategy in deciding! Quite simply the lowest home loan in most cases should be the one that you start to pay out first. The reason for this is that although you are charging interest, there are no payments being made back to The Syndicate until the loan has been completely paid out from the bank. This is because on a bank home loan that a borrower takes out for $100,000 he/she is already paying back about $650 p/m. It may be difficult to then pay $650 to the bank plus an extra $200 p/m to The Syndicate as a loan repayment as well as the standard monthly Syndicate payments. With fear of repeating myself if they did have surplus money they are better off paying that to the bank's home loan and clearing that as quickly as possible, thereby allowing them to start paying The Syndicate loan back even sooner. Table 9 is an example of a Syndicate Home Loan Account.

Table 9 Example of Syndicate Home Loan Account

Date	Name of Borrower: Frank Smart / Description or Comment	Loan Amount	Payment Amount	Interest Rate 6.5%pa	Balance
3/05/09	Payment to Home Loan	10,000			10,000.00
31/05/09	interest			54.16	10,054.16
30/06/09	interest			54.46	10108.62
31/07/09	interest			54.75	10163.37
14/08/09	Payment to Home Loan	5,000			15163.37
31/08/09	interest			82.13	15245.50
30/09/09	Interest			82.57	15328.07
Cross Check Totals	**Loan amounts – payments+ Interest= Balance**	**15,000**	**0**	**328.07**	**$15328.07 it Balances with above**

The columns here are self explanatory and the same as for The Syndicate **Personal Loan** sheet. In the interest rate column show the interest rate as either per annum or per month and when entering the amounts use cents. At the bottom do your cross-check to make sure you have done your maths right. Generally there will be no payments until the original loan with the bank has been paid out in full.

For The Syndicate member whose loan has been paid out, although they are accumulating interest and it looks like they owe more each month, in fact they are not. As previously discussed, this is due to the Mathematical Law of Distribution. Refer back to table 7 and then take a look at table 10 below.

Table 10 comparing a split loan

Original loan	payment	interest@6%pa	balance	New Balance
$100,000	$600	$500	$99,900	$99,900
		Original Loan – payment + Interest = balance		
New Loan	**payment**	**interest@6%pa**	**balance**	**New Balance**
$80,000	$600	$400	$79,800 Down $200	$99,900
Syndicate Loan				
$20,000	0	$100	$20100 Up $100	

Original Loan – payment + Interest = balance

As you can see the new balance is the same for both loans whether it is one loan or split into two loans. The new loan for $80,000 will go down quicker now, so it will be paid out from the bank sooner. Remember that for every dollar The Syndicate earns it's a dollar that the bank doesn't get as well as a dollar that The Syndicate can put to good use. In addition, of all the interest that you as a member pay over the life of The Syndicate, if there are 4 members you will get ¼ of that back and if there are 6 you will get ⅙ back. The same applies when someone uses the money that you have put into The Syndicate - they are then charged interest of which you will get a share back too. However insignificant it may seem, it's certainly a lot more than the banks are giving back!! ☺

The Syndicate Expense Account

The **Syndicate Expense Account** was set up for ease and fun. Once operating, I wondered how we ever managed before it existed. We found that during the course of running The Syndicate there were some ongoing expenses that needed to be accounted for. For example, we were charged cheque fees (these days it would be Account Fees of $5 or $10 a month). There were also other expenses along the way like books, paper, and a white board (for our meetings). It did not seem fair that one person was supplementing these group expenses all the time, so we decided these charges needed to be accounted for and split amongst us evenly.

We then set up a loan account book (except we called it the Expense Account Book). We didn't lose the plot and start charging ourselves interest on the expenses, we used it just to keep track of them, writing in what the expenses were and what the running total was. Then at the end of each quarter we took the running total and divided it by number of members and transferred that amount to each members loan account evenly. It might have been only $50 - $60 dollars in total.

We were a family Syndicate and quite often found over the years that each of us needed similar household items or tools (we were all quite the "Home Handy Man" type…or at least we thought we were and some proved better than others!) One of the first things we needed (or perhaps I should say wanted) was a trailer. They were relatively cheap in those days (can't believe I just said that!) at around $400. So we decided that The Syndicate would buy that as an expense! We were good were we not? We also bought a cement mixer, a drop saw, a chain saw and a few other tools as well.

All the tools we bought were recognised as belonging to The Syndicate and not to any member individually. They were held at one or the others place and borrowed back and forth as needed. It worked just great, I really didn't need a chainsaw all the time and even if I did buy it myself, I would have been asked if it could be borrowed. So it made good sense to buy it jointly, plus we had a record of when we bought it and where it was etc.

Then we realised how a good idea can evolve into a great idea. After the chainsaw was used one weekend it needed a new chain and instead of arguing about who used it last or did what with it, it became the expense of The Syndicate and instead of one person paying $50 for a new chain we let the **Syndicate Expense Account** pay for it and divided the expense evenly at the end of the quarter. The same was true for the trailer registration, when it became due for renewal it went on the **Syndicate Expense Account** as did the puncture repair and the new motor for the cement mixer.

At the end of the quarter (you may choose to do it ½ yearly or not at all) we divided the balance of the **Syndicate Expense Account** amongst us evenly and put it on to our **Syndicate Loan Accounts**. Sure someone could have paid for it outright or a few of us could have paid their share as a cash payment at the end of the quarter instead of it going on their loan, but for those who could not afford it at the time it was a blessing, and those that could afford it just paid extra off their loan when the time was right for them. See table 11 for an example of the Expense Account.

Table 11 Example of Expense Account

Date	Expense Account / Expense Description or Comment	Expense Amount	Payment Amount	Balance
3/05/09	Cement Mixer	200		200
15/05/09	Bought Calculator Canon	60		260
13/06/09	Bought faint ruled a/c books	16		277
23/07/09	Bought Trailer	400		677
14/08/09	Paid for Puncture	14		690
31/08/09	Payment made by members		690[2]	0
Cross Check Totals	**Expense amounts – payments= Balance**	690	690	$0 it Balances with above

The Expense account is optional. It worked very well for us in the purchase of necessities and extras alike. It allowed us to have access to things that we could not have each afforded to buy separately. It still has its place even if it is for the day to day running expenses of The Syndicate like printers, toner cartridges, whiteboard markers, etc. You will be surprised what pops up from time to time.

---

[2] Each Member (6) would have had $115 put against their Syndicate Loan Account

The Syndicate Investment Account

Remember, The Syndicate needs to think like a bank, and a bank continually investigates different ways to make an income. It may all seem slow to start off with, but hazarding repetition I again remind you that every dollar that The Syndicate makes is a dollar the bank does not get and therefore comes back to you and the other Syndicate members.

So what is this product about? "Investment!" I hear you say, and you're precisely correct. Although the primary role of The Syndicate is to pay off your loans and provide financial self-sufficiency for all involved, there will come a time when one - if not all - members of The Syndicate will have surpluses of cash. (I know it might seem unbelievable now, but you'll be surprised!!)

In the normal chain of events a bank will receive money from deposits that you and everybody else makes to the bank and that money is in turn loaned out to other borrowers. You then earn a whopping 2-3% p.a. and they loan it out at 9-11% p.a. as a personal loan, making around 7-8% on your money! That's business. The Syndicate needs to do the same – just follow the lead of the banks.

It may only be one member with some extra money, and you don't have to wait until everybody has the same amount spare. It may come about by way of a tax return or inheritance, and although you could pay it off your personal loan or home loan (if you still have one), you may not wish to. This could be for any number of reasons but perhaps because once you have paid it off the bank loan, you will not be able to redraw it. Alternatively, as The Syndicate matures and has paid off one or two home loans and these members have paid it back in full they may have accumulated some surplus this way too. Regardless of how it arises, the question is what to do with it?

It is here that the **Syndicate Investment Account** jumps into action. Let's look at a real life situation. Say that Frank leaves his job to go to a competitor and is starting the following Monday. The company that he currently works for dismisses Frank immediately because of conflict of interest. Frank is paid monthly so they pay him one months pay in lieu of notice, plus holiday leave owing and pro-rata of long service leave. So after tax Frank takes home $11,000 (nice pay for the month!). Now because Frank is starting his new job on Monday and does not intend to take any holidays, he keeps a little spending money and has $10,000 surplus. If he invests it with the bank in a 12 month fixed term deposit he may earn 5-6% p.a. at most. So why not invest it back into The Syndicate instead? The Syndicate can then loan it out as a **Syndicate Personal Loan** to one or two of the members and charge them 12% p.a. and then as an incentive pay the would-be investor 9% p.a. (that's 3 or 4% more than they would have received from the bank, plus it's tax-free!)[3]. Don't forget the investor has made 9% on his/her money and the syndicate has earned the other 3% which when divided amongst the members later means the investor will also get an extra ¾ % depending howmany members are in the syndicate.

Of course there are some traps to be aware of! You would not have the money invested with The Syndicate paying 9% p.a. to the investor and only loaning it out at 6% p.a. to the borrower - The Syndicate would be losing 3%! Also, the money would only be loaned to someone that can afford to pay it back without financial distress. Finally, the investor would have to understand that if they invested it to be loaned to a Syndicate member they may have to give at least 3-4 months notice for The Syndicate to be able to pay it back. This would of course depend on the cash flow of The Syndicate – meaning that if there are a couple of loans that are being paid back, then

---

[3] The tax side of the whole Syndicate is not complicated, as a member you are not earning money more like saving it! The interest earned directly from the bank on the Syndicate Savings Account Balance should be split evenly and declared on your tax return. Although this is how it worked for us, everyone's situation is different and so you should get an opinion from a tax professional.

it's quite possible that there is around $5000 coming back into The Syndicate each month.

There is also the option that the investor may pay the money in and one of the members pays it of their credit card with the understanding that if at short notice the investor needed their money back then the member that borrowed it could get a cash advance. These are all ideas and ideas only. How you decide to work out the final rates and rules is up to your members. But it is important to be fair, and just as important to be consistent with what you decide. It would cause arguments if you loaned money to one member at say 12% p.a. then loaned to another at say 15% p.a. whilst paying interest to two investors at the same rates. Likewise paying two investors at different rates would cause tension too.

There will be times over the life of The Syndicate where interest rates on a national or global level will fluctuate and The Syndicate will need to accommodate those fluctuations. We have seen interest rates soar and we have seen them tumble over a very short time frame[4]. Remember you are friends/family and the first rule is you must all agree. There is never, nor ever will be room for private negotiations between two members, that is a sure recipe for disaster!

Setting up of the **Syndicate Investment Account** is similar in most cases to the **Syndicate Loan Account** except obviously it is a positive amount and you are earning interest instead of being charged it. See table 12

---

[4] At the time of writing official interest rates fell almost 5% in 12 months.

Table 12 Example of the Syndicate Investment

Date	Name of Investor: Frank Smart	Investment Amount	Withdrawn Amount	Interest	Balance
	Description or Comment			Rate 12%pa	
3/05/09	Amount Invested/deposited	10,000			10,000.00
31/05/09	interest			100.00	10,100.00
30/06/09	interest			101.00	10,201.00
31/07/09	interest			102.01	10,303.01
14/08/09	Investment returned/withdrawn		5,000		5,303.01
31/08/09	interest			53.02	5,356.03
30/09/09	Interest			53.55	5,409.58
Cross Check Totals	Investment amounts – Withdrawals+ interest= Balance	10,000	5,000	409.58	$5,409.58 it Balances with above

The columns are self explanatory and are similar to The Syndicate Personal Loan sheet, in the interest rate column show the interest rate as either per annum or per month. When entering the amounts use cents. At the bottom do your cross-check to make sure you have done your maths right.

When the investor makes a withdrawal from his investment account the money would be paid to him directly as an internet funds transfer. The investor may ask to have the money paid to their Syndicate Account Book or to their **Syndicate Loan Account** (if they have one). You may be asking why would they have a **Syndicate Loan Account** and also have a **Syndicate Investment Account**.

Let's say that Mark is the investor and he already has a **Syndicate Personal Loan** of $15,000, but now due to a small windfall has $5000 to invest. If he pays it off the **Syndicate Personal Loan** he may not be able to get it out again or not straight away at least (when you are allocating the money for different loans it would only be fair to give each person an opportunity to borrow the money instead of letting just one or two members borrow it). So by Mark investing it with The Syndicate instead he can invest it for six months stipulating that he will need it back after that time has elapsed. If The Syndicate cash flow supports this need then he can invest it for six months, with the security of knowing that he still has the money. Plus Mark and The Syndicate both make some money in interest.

It's worth pointing out that the money is just that - money - and when it is invested or loaned out the agreed interest rate is more important than to whom it is loaned. The loan it is used for will be unanimously voted by The Syndicate, not nominated by the investor. The investor can only nominate the market rate they are prepared to invest at. There will be instances where money is loaned out at 6% p.a. (home loan) and some at 15% p.a. (personal loan), and some will be in the bank only earning 2% p.a. (hopefully not much – it should be utilised for loaning).

Just like a bank that lends money for a personal loan at 14% p.a. fixed rate and then interest rates drop to 12% p.a., they still get their 14% p.a. Likewise if they (the banks) lend money for a home loan at 6.5% p.a. fixed and it climbs to 8% p.a. they are losing 1.5% (not happy Jan!). Its worth mentioning these day most loans are variable that is to they follow the market if the rates go up so do theirs if they go down so do theirs (most times), where as fixed rates are just that fixed for the term of the loan. The same applies when you decide to invest for the purpose of lending to other Syndicate members, you don't have control of how it is used, and have agreed to a fixed rate return at the beginning of the investment. How the money is used and who it is loaned to will depend on the needs of The Syndicate members at the time. Just keep the big picture in sight with The Syndicate, be flexible but treat it like a business and be fair. The secret that we discovered is that you can make it good fun and rewarding without imposing all the rules like the bank or finance companies do. If somebody is late making a payment you don't charge them a $30.00 late fee, or a $50 redraw fee, or a $150 security fee.

The Syndicate Medical Account

The **Syndicate Medical Account** is not for the faint hearted. If a Syndicate member or a member of his or her family has a current serious medical condition then this is definitely not a replacement for a proper medical fund. However that being said, think about how much money you and your family spend on medical expenses throughout the year like the doctors, dentist, prescriptions, spectacles, contact lenses, acupuncture, chiropractic, psychology- I'm sure you get the picture without me quoting the statistics. If you are in a health fund that's great, but lets look at the big picture (keeping in mind the following figures are just a rough approximation to illustrate my point).

Direct Restorations	
Metal filling - one surface (511)	$45.65
Metal filling - three surfaces (513)	$66.25
Adhesive filling 1 surface (front) (521)	$48.65
Adhesive filling 3 surfaces (front) (523)	$68.45
Adhesive filling 1 surface (back) (531)	$51.00

Figure 1 Dental rebates

Say you go to the dentist and he fills one tooth (I am not going to be technical here) and charges you $200.00 - ouch! That hurts but it's ok because you have extras cover in your medical fund which covers you…right? You put your claim in and you only get back $45.65 - now that just leaves a bad taste in your mouth - you're $155 out of pocket! You and your family are in quite good health and only go twice a year at a rate of $200 per visit, factoring a refund of about $45 each time. Now for the privilege of having that extras cover you paid $1000 p.a., then you had to contribute maybe $155 to bridge the gap so all up it cost you around $1300 p.a. to get back $90.00.

Sometimes it's not so much about how much they will give you back per visit i.e. 30-40% but the refund limits that apply. Glasses for example you may only get 70% back to a maximum of $180 per year per person on lenses and frames, not 70% of your total cost). My most recent lenses and frames cost me $700 in total (and they're not designer, fancy or top-of-the-range). So I would be out of pocket over $500.00. The tables above and below (Figures 1 & 2) are from a comparison web site in 2009[5] and are for a couple with "intermediate" extras cover at around $85 p/m or $1020 per year. Notice that there is also a waiting period of 6 months for optical!

Ancillary Service	Rebate	Financial year Limit		Waiting Period
Optical				
		per person	per family	6 months
Frames, Single lenses, Bi-foca, Multi-focal and Contact Lenses	$180	$180	$450	
Repairs to frames or lenses (payable for scripted sight correcting products only)	$40			

Figure 2 Optical Rebate

http://www.iselect.com.au

I want to stress and repeat the first statement in this chapter, which is, if a Syndicate member or a member of his or her family has a current serious medical condition then this is definitely not a replacement for a proper medical fund. But what you could do is have hospital cover which would protect you from the cost of hospitalisation caused from major accidents and/or illnesses, and have your own private and I mean literally private extras cover via the **Syndicate Medical Account**.

---

[5] This information was correct at the time of publishing (2009).

This is how it works. You work out how much you are paying per year (or would pay if you were in an extras fund) and divide that by 12 to give you the monthly amount. Let's say its $900 p.a. divided by 12 = $75 per month, now lets also say that in your Syndicate there are 6 people so that is 6 x $75 pm or $450 each month available. As this is a medical fund you have a separate savings account for this and a **Syndicate Medical Account Book** that will keep track of deposits by each Syndicate member as well as payments out of the Account (this is strictly for accounting purposes only).

When a Syndicate member or his/her family member goes to the chiropractor for an adjustment they pay the bill and get a receipt, the member then provides that to The Syndicate who pays out the agreed percentage.

The agreed percentage can be whatever is agreed by The Syndicate members at the start - it can be 75%, 80%, 90% or even 100% of the bill (not too many funds will do that!). The interesting thing is that even if your Syndicate pays 100% you will still be in front. I would suggest that when you first start off that the reimbursement is only 75% for the first year or so until you build up some financial reserves in the **Syndicate Medical Account**.

How you decide to pay this monthly amount into the **Syndicate Medical Account** is up to the members. One way is to charge it against the members Syndicate Personal Loan Account each month. The **Syndicate Medical Account** will be in some ways similar to the expense account in that it will not incur or pay any interest.

As the amount continues to grow in the **Syndicate Medical Account** you may decide to have an upper limit for the account to reach, perhaps around $5000. This may only take 12 months depending on how many Syndicate members there are and how much you decide to pay in. Once you reach the $5000 you wait for it to get to $6000 and then withdraw $1000, thereby returning the balance to the $5000 maximum. The

$1000 can then be divided evenly and paid back into The Syndicate main account and used somewhere else, a member may decide to pay that off their loan or to start up a **Syndicate Investment Account**, admittedly it may only be $150 or so but it's a start! The bigger picture is that you now have a reserve of $5000 in an account and your medical bills are being paid at the same time! The maximum held in reserve is for your Syndicate to decide. The following Table 13 shows you how the **Syndicate Medical Account** could be set up.

Table 13 Example of Medical Account

Date	Medical Account Description or Comment	Payment in	Payment out	Balance
3/05/09	Members payment in	450		450
1/06/09	Members payment in	450		900
1/07/09	Members payment in	450		1350
23/07/09	Payment out receipt 16565		45	1305
1/08/09	Members payment in	450		1755
1/09/09	Members payment in	450		2205
12/09/09	Payment out receipt GB2489		195	2010
15/09/09	Payment out receipt 14		12	1998
1/10/09	Members payment in	450		2448
Cross Check Totals	Payments in – payments out = Balance	2,700	252	$2448 it Balances with above

The columns are self explanatory. Again don't forget to cross-check at the bottom.

Even though you have been reimbursed from the **Syndicate Medical Account**, your medical expenses may still be claimable against your tax if you meet the Tax Office's upper limit for medical expenses incurred. You should seek professional financial advice from your accountant on these matters.

The Whole Picture

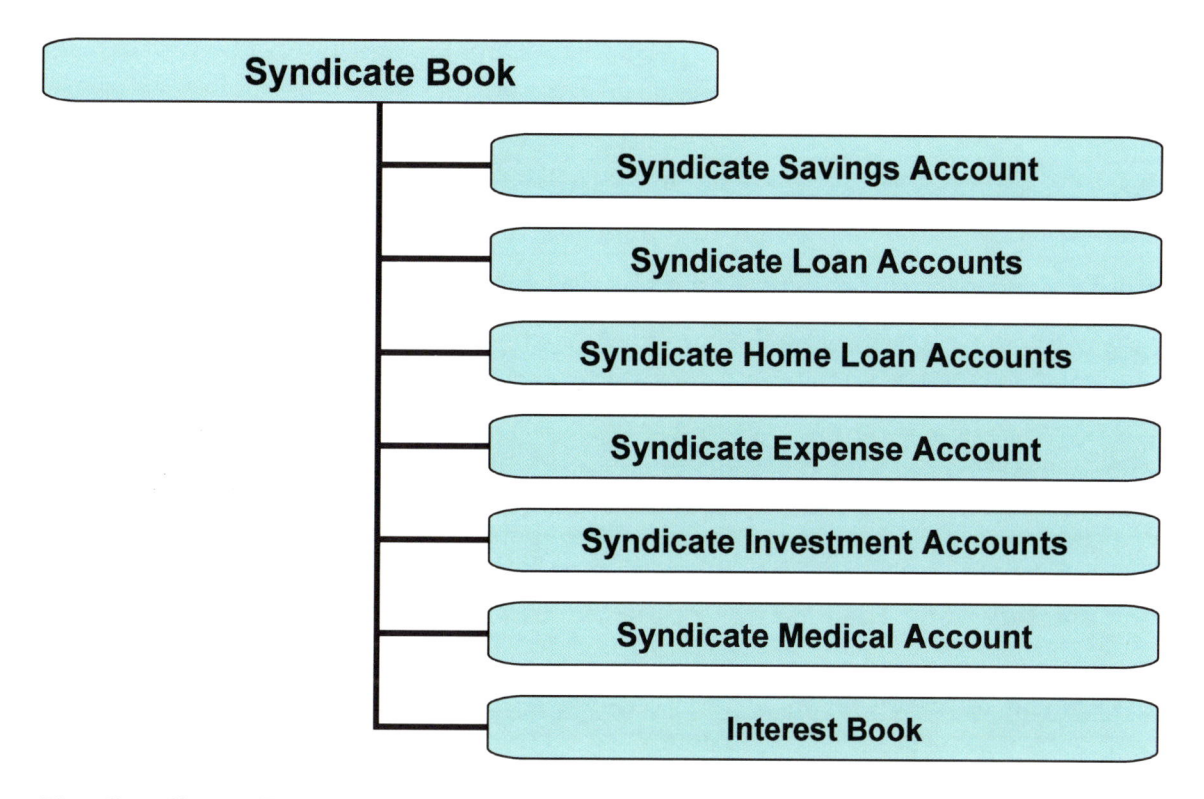

```
Syndicate Book
   ├── Syndicate Savings Account
   ├── Syndicate Loan Accounts
   ├── Syndicate Home Loan Accounts
   ├── Syndicate Expense Account
   ├── Syndicate Investment Accounts
   ├── Syndicate Medical Account
   └── Interest Book
```

The Syndicate Total Value =

All Savings Accounts + All Loan Accounts + Expense – Medical Account – Investment Account.

The Syndicate Total Interest =

All Savings Account Interest + All Loan Account Interest – All Investment Account Interest.

The Syndicate book =

Syndicates Total Value – Syndicate Total Interest.

The above looks confusing but its not – just do one step at a time!

One of the most important tasks is the balancing of the **Syndicate Books**. As you would expect, every dollar and cent must be accounted for. Interest is always calculated at the end of the month on each account book.

Before we can balance The Syndicate there is a book that we need to create to help us keep track of The Syndicate and to help balance The Syndicate. This book is called the **Interest Book** and as the name suggests it is for the sole purpose of tracking all the interest charged, received and/or paid by The Syndicate each month. We do this because it is much easier to see the true figures when you separate the interest from all the loans and investments. It is not hard to understand that the total value of The Syndicate is everything added together – that is loans, investments, medical, and interest. If you want to know just what you have contributed in Syndicate payments alone you would take the total Syndicate value and minus all the interest paid, charged and received. The Interest Book could look similar to the following Table 14:

Table 14 Example of Interest Book

Date	comments	Saving Interest	Loan interest	Investment Interest ** (minus amounts)	Balance
31/01/09	No investment interest	10	65	0	75
28/02/09		23	95	-50	143
31/03/09		45	120	-50.50	257.50
30/04/09	No savings interest	0	170	-50.50	377.00*
Cross check	**Totals for cross check**	**78**	**450**	**-151**	**Balances $377.00***

** Notice that the investment interest is a negative amount. That is because effectively The Syndicate is paying the interest out. Still do the cross-check at the bottom though.

The Check List

Therefore to balance the books you must do the following-

- At the end of each month finalise all transactions in and out of The Syndicate
- Make sure all transactions have been recorded in the appropriate **Syndicate Books**
- Make sure all balances have been cross-checked at the end of the month (rule off page if necessary)
- Add all The Syndicate loan balances for each member together and record the total **(Total Syndicate Loans)**
    - Add all the interest received from savings accounts and <u>bank</u> investment accounts (if any)
    - Add all the interest <u>charged</u> for the month on loans and record the total in the Interest Book
- Add all The Syndicate Investment balances for each member together and record the total **(Total Syndicate Investments).**
    - Add all the interest <u>paid</u> for the month on investments and record the total in the Interest Book
    - Add the total of all **Syndicate Books** which will include Savings Account, all Syndicate Loans and **Syndicate Expense Account**
- From this balance subtract the total of all the investment account balances (if you have any)
- From this balance subtract **Syndicate Medical Account** (if you have one)

If you have done all of the above correctly you now have all the information you need to balance the **Syndicate Books**.

The Syndicate Total Value =

All Savings Accounts + All Loan Accounts + Expense – Medical Account – Investment Account.

The Syndicate Total Interest =

All Savings Account Interest + All Loan Account Interest – All Investment Account Interest.

The Syndicate book =

Syndicates Total Value – Syndicate Total Interest. (**This is the most important one and is used for the balancing of The Syndicate)

The idea is to make sure that you have accounted for all the money, and in reality some of it is done as you go like the cross-checking at the bottom of the various loans, investments, expense account etc. When you are sure that the figures are correct, then you add it all up. Once you have the entire amount, the interest is then subtracted. The result should be what you have paid in to The Syndicate in the form of the weekly Syndicate amounts (the payment you each started making from the beginning and should have kept up consistently since).

I'm sure there are other ways to explain The Syndicate balancing process, for instance accountants would divide it in to debit and credits, assets, liabilities, and equities. In fact you could set up a whole chart of accounts. If you can do that and it works well then please do so. This book is not designed to be highly technical but simply to introduce you to the concepts involved and some basic ways to make it work for you and the people you invite to share your Syndicate. Your individual processes and decisions about how you apply these concepts are completely yours.

I have developed an Excel spreadsheet to help keep track of interest and transactions. It is quite simple to use and you may have already purchased it with this book. However, if you are good with Excel perhaps you can create your own or maybe you'd just like to use pen and paper. Just remember to follow your instinct and common sense – making The Syndicate work for your members is more important than trying to follow each of my suggestions to the letter.

What If…?

There are two common issues which may arise in the life of The Syndicate, as follows:

1. At the time your Syndicate started, one of the potential members may not have been old enough/ could not afford it/ was overseas / was sceptical. But they have now seen it working and want to join! How does this happen say 2 or 3 years down the track? Well it's easy! All you need to do is find what the total value of The Syndicate is and divide it by the current number of members. How easy is that? For example you have all (6 of you) put in, in the form of Syndicate payments only, a total of $37440 over the 3 years, in addition to which you have earned $3500 in interest, so that's a total of $40940. Therefore each of you has put in $6823.33, so for every extra person that wants to join they have to put in $6823.33 each.

   So let's say that Brendan could not afford the $50 per week at the start of The Syndicate, and although he can now afford the regular contributions, he doesn't have over $6000 on hand now to "buy in". So The Syndicate gives him a loan for that amount instead. Here's the tricky part, that amount is made up of Syndicate payments and interest so if you divide the $37440 by 6 equals $6240 and $3500 divide by 6 = $583.33 is interest. You add a column in The Syndicate **Book** and add Brendan's name and increase the total by $6240. Then you go to the interest book and add the interest of $583.33 as a separate amount, just as you would at the end of the month for the other interest amounts. This whole process is the only way that you can keep a fair and equal share in The Syndicate for everyone. Of course if for some reason a member was leaving The Syndicate, perhaps going overseas to live and did not want to continue, then you could do the exact opposite. That is, find The Syndicate total value divided by the number of members and give that person their share, first deducting any loans that they may have, then working out the Interest part and writing it up in The Syndicate **Book** and the Interest book (as a deduction of course).

Table 15 Typical Syndicate Books when adding a new person

Date	Mark	Karen	Frank	John	New Person	Comment	Balance
Oct 5	40	40	40	40		payment	23360
Oct 12	40	40	40	40		payment	23520
Oct 19	40	40	40	40		payment	23680
Oct 26	40	40	40	40		payment	23840
Nov 2	40	40	40	40		payment	24000
Nov 9	40	40	40	40		payment	24160
Nov 16	40	40	40	40		payment	24320
Nov 23	40	40	40	40		payment	24480
Nov 30	40	40	40	40		payment	24640
Dec 7	40	40	40	40		payment	24800
Dec 14	40	40	40	40		payment	24960
Dec 21	40	40	40	40	6280 (6240+40)	**New Member**	31400
Dec 28	40	40	40	40	40	payment	31600
							↓↓↓↓↓↓
Balance	6320	6320	6320	6320	6320	→→→	31600 this is the cross balance check

Table 16 Typical Interest Book when adding a new person

Date	comments	Saving Interest	Loan interest	Investment Interest ** (minus amounts)	Balance
31/8/09	No investment interest	10	65	0	3211.5
30/9/09		23	95	-50	3279.5
31/10/09		45	120	-50.50	3385.50
30/11/09	No savings interest	0	170	-50.50	3500.00
21/12/09	New member	583.33			4460.33*
Cross check	Totals for cross check	755.00	5155.78	-1450.45	Balances $4460.33*

2. At some stage you may decide to close The Syndicate down, which could be for a multitude of reasons but the most likely (and exciting!) reason is it's fulfilled its purpose. All you need to do is again find The Syndicate's total value and divide it by the number of members. That will then become their share. However, if a member has loans still outstanding he/she would need to apply their loan balance to their share value and then either receive the balance or pay the extra in. If for some reason there is still an outstanding amount then that member would have to go and get a personal loan from a bank so that they can finalise their Syndicate loan.

Hey Presto – You've Got Yourself a Syndicate!

I hope this book has changed the way you consider your finances, and given you some inspiration to do things differently from now on. I hope it has not left you thinking that I hate financial institutions, or that I think you should either. I see them as a very necessary (sometimes evil) requirement. Let's face it, without them you wouldn't have been able to buy that house or boat or computer in the first place! Just as we could not survive without them they certainly would not be able to survive without us (although they do act like it sometimes!)

Also, please don't make the mistake of putting this to one side and thinking it could not really change your life or financial future. Just consider for a moment that if you have a $350,000 loan at 6% p.a. and you pay $2098 p/m over 30 years then you pay just over $755,000 in total. That means $350,000 for the house and $405,000 to the bank. I can hear the *"k-ching"* from here! Oh and don't forget to multiply that by 6 if there are 6 members in your Syndicate with similar loans. This is of course not to the mention the 'incidental' amount of interest to be made from The Syndicate paying out credit cards, personal loans and car loans along the way (at double the interest rate for a house).

So find your family, friends and work mates, have a chat, have a meeting, open up a bank account, and start saving some money! Get yourselves a bank balance and loan it out to yourselves. Charge some interest, and let it compound. Loan it out some more and let it grow faster. Have The Syndicate pay some of your larger bills like rates, car registration and home insurance and stop living pay-to-pay.

Join forces and buy some tools to share to save some more money, put a little extra in and put it to one side and call it your medical fund. When you go to the dentist instead of paying $240 and getting $100 back now get back $180 - $200 because you as a small group decide how much to refund.

If you get some surplus money, invest it with your Syndicate and get twice as much interest that the banks pay. As the money accumulates - and it will - start to pay off your home loans with no fees, no break fees, no legal fees, no search fees, no withdrawal fees, no contracts.

Become self sufficient, take the stress away, have some money in the bank (or Syndicate), have some fun and LIVE!

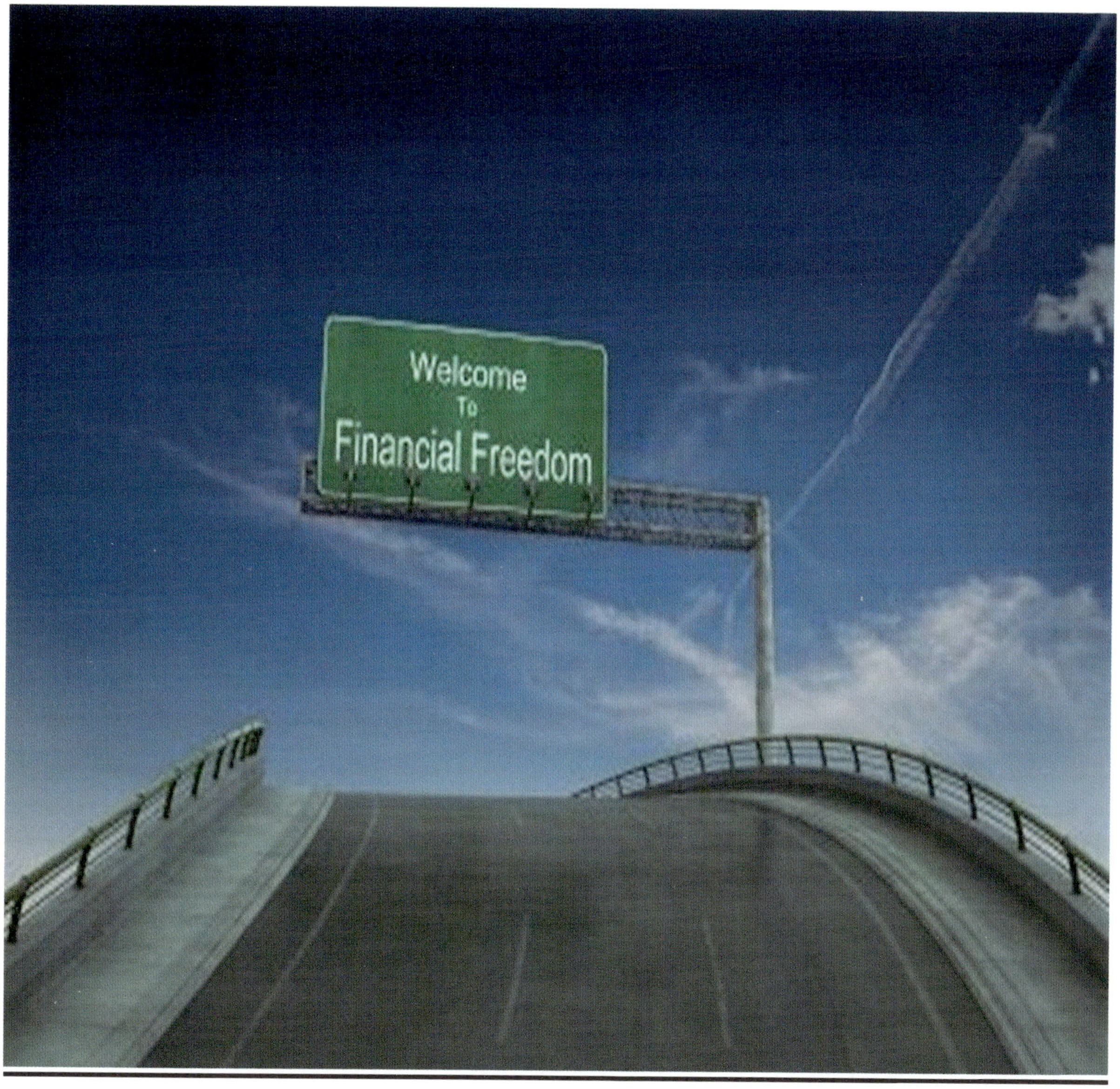
Welcome
To
Financial Freedom

Appendix

Table 17 Syndicate Books sample page

Date	Name 1	Name 2	Name 3	Name 4	Comment	Balance

Table 18 Personal Loan Account sample page

Date	Description	Loan Amount	Interest ___% p/m	Payment	Balance owing

Table 18 Home Loan Account sample page

Date	Name of Borrower: Description or Comment	Loan Amount	Payment Amount	Interest Rate %pa	Balance

Table 20 Expense Account sample page

Date	Expense Account Expense Description or Comment	Expense Amount	Payment Amount	Balance

Table 21 Syndicate Investment sample page

Date	Name of Investor: Description or Comment	Investment Amount	Withdrawn Amount	Interest Rate___%pa	Balance

Table 22 Syndicate Medical Account sample page

Date	Medical Account Description or Comment	Payment in	Payment out	Balance

Table 23 Sample of Interest Book

Date	comments	Saving Interest	Loan interest	Investment Interest ** (minus amounts)	Balance

Edition	6.0
Written	2009
Revised	2013
Published	2009, 2011, 2013
Author	Les Field
Editor	Marea Ford

The Author can be contacted by email Author@thesyndicatebook.com with any questions or suggestions (all are welcome).

The Author has produced an easy to use Microsoft Excel spread sheet that is available. It will carry out all aspects of The Syndicate from Syndicate books to Loan accounts and interest calculations, including balancing of the various accounts automatically. Available by request $30.00**
www.thesyndicatebook.com

Made in the USA
Charleston, SC
04 May 2013